Sports Illustrated
DOG TRAINING

By Ken Norman

D1548104

The Sports Illustrated Library

BOOKS ON TEAM SPORTS

Baseball	Basketball	Football	Ice Hockey
Soccer	Volleyball		

BOOKS ON INDIVIDUAL SPORTS

Badminton	Golf	Skiing
Fencing	Horseback Riding	Squash
Fly Fishing	The Shotgun	Tennis
Gaited Riding	Shotgun Sports	Track and Field: Running Events

BOOKS ON WATER SPORTS

Better Boating	Junior Sailing	Swimming
Diving	Small Boat Sailing	

SPECIAL BOOKS

Dog Training	Safe Driving

𝒳. ᴺ·

Sports Illustrated
DOG
TRAINING

BY THE EDITORS OF
SPORTS ILLUSTRATED

J. B. LIPPINCOTT COMPANY
Philadelphia and New York

U.S. Library of Congress Cataloging in Publication Data

Sports illustrated (Chicago)
   Sports illustrated dog training.

   (Sports illustrated library)
   First ed. cataloged in 1960 under title: Book of dog
training.
   1. Dogs—Training. I. Title.
SF431.S66   1972   636.7'088   72-3179
ISBN-0-397-00906-2
ISBN-0-397-00907-0 (pbk.)

Copyright © 1958, 1959, 1972, by Time Inc.

Revised Edition

All rights reserved

Printed in the United States of America

Photographs from *Sports Illustrated,* © Time Inc.

Cover photograph: George P. Berger

Photographs on pages 8, 42 and 62: Hanson Carroll, S.I.

Photograph on page 61: Gerry Cranham, S.I.

Photographs on pages 86-95: Evelyn M. Shafer

Contents

5. THE RUGGED RETRIEVERS

By James A. Cowie with Virginia Kraft
Illustrations by Anthony Ravielli

6. THE POINTING DOGS

By Richard S. Johns
Illustrations by Arthur Shilstone

7. A GALLERY OF POPULAR FIELD DOGS

1
The Family Dog
By Lois Meistrell

ONE of the most delightful—and perplexing—of all family problems begins when you bring home a new puppy. What happens from that moment on is up to you—his arrival can mean chaos and confusion, disrupted schedules and distraught tempers; or it can mean pleasure and companionship for every member of the family. Here Lois Meistrell of Pownal, Vermont, who has worked with all breeds of dogs in her 25 years as both amateur and professional trainer, tells you how you can train your new puppy to be a rewarding and well-behaved addition to the family group.

INITIAL ADJUSTMENTS

A puppy, like a baby, is a bewildered creature in a strange world. Until he feels secure in his new environment he will

9

either fear or fight it. First he needs a place of his own—and this should *not* be a lonely cellar or garage. Put him in a wire cage. Lined with a towel, it will double as a bed. In a cage like this he can see, be seen and be near you without getting underfoot. Speak to him whenever possible. He won't understand what you say, but he will understand the tones you use. For the first week move his cage into your bedroom at night. Then he will know you are safely nearby, and instead of whining he will sleep.

During the day and evening before bedtime, surround the wire cage with playpen-sized wire fencing or buy four 4-foot-square panels at a hardware or department store, or a mail-order or pet shop, and hook them together. Cover the entire floor of the playpen with paper and place the cage, with the door open, in it.

This unattractive grouping in one corner of your kitchen is not forever; but for the present it provides the pup with

A wire cage doubles as a bed and a carrying case, permits the pup to see and be seen and to adjust to surroundings.

A housebreaking pen can be set up in the kitchen or the yard. Put newspaper in the pen with the pup. If, at first, he fails to use the paper, reprimand him with a stern "No" until an association is established.

freedom to move about, and keeps him out of your way. It also hastens his housebreaking without constant attention on your part.

Since dogs do not like to soil where they sleep, the pup will come out of his towel-covered cage to relieve himself. By having the entire surface of the pen covered with paper, he has no choice but to soil on it, so he is always right. You will find that within a short time he will be going to one or two spots each time and leaving the rest of the paper untouched. When he reaches this stage, remove the excess paper and leave it only in the spots he uses. You have already, with very little effort, got him into the habit of leaving his "home" and soiling away from it.

When he is old enough to go outside, place another pen right outside the back door and put him in it. It then becomes an extension of what he is familiar with indoors. He leaves the house and goes to a similar pen, which is different only in that it has a different surface. Let him explore it and wait until he uses it before bringing him back in.

The pen has other advantages. By remaining in it, the pup never has the opportunity to chew electric cords or children's toys, jump on furniture or steal food. While you will need to train him not to do these things later on, you will at least start that training from scratch, instead of having to correct bad habits first.

Once he is housebroken and well-mannered, you can use the sides of the inside pen to enlarge the one outdoors. Having a larger area for him avoids the necessity of walking him in the street every time he has to go.

Since puppies relieve themselves eight to ten times a day, this alternative is a time-consuming nuisance. Even when the dog is grown it becomes a burdensome task late at night and in bad weather. Walk the dog on the street, by all means, when you have the time and the inclination, but don't make it a daily "must." The average dog gets plenty of exercise in his own home and back yard.

The alternative of taking the dog to a vacant lot—or, worse, a public park—and letting him run free can cost you a lot. You may lose the dog by theft or injury; he may pick up something harmful left by stray animals, in which case you will end up with a large veterinary bill; or you may get a summons for disobeying local ordinances about loose dogs. Regulations are becoming more and more severe, and the clamor, frequently justified, by non-dog owners about the mess created by irresponsible dog owners will probably make them even stricter.

New puppies are most likely to be hurt, physically and psychologically, by overeager children. Immature dogs are fragile—their bones break easily and internal injuries often result from good-natured roughhousing. If you have a young child and a new pup, each must learn to respect as well as enjoy the other. Begin by teaching your child to pick up the pup with one hand supporting his chest, the other his hindquarters. In this way the pup cannot squirm out of the child's grip or twist into a harmful position. Remind the child to talk to the puppy so that he will be at

The proper way to hold a new pup.

To pick up a puppy correctly, put your hands under his chest and hindquarters, distributing his weight and preventing him from falling.

ease. In play, discourage quick lunges at the dog. Any movement from behind—especially rapid movement—frightens a puppy, because he doesn't see or understand it. Let the child bring himself down to the dog's level by sitting on the floor and waiting; sooner or later natural curiosity will attract pup to child. In this way the dog will learn to expect comfort and approval rather than harm from his young owner.

Playing with the pup can be harmful and frightening if a child lunges at him. Wait for the pup on his level, permit him to approach voluntarily.

14

Training to the Lead

From the moment a new puppy enters the home, he should learn to wear a small leather collar. One with bells will help you keep track of his whereabouts. As soon as he becomes used to it (this will take two or three days), attach a light lead and let him drag it about. This helps reduce any wildness or fear many young pups show when first on a lead. After a few days, pick up one end of the lead and hold it loosely while you walk around the yard or home. Don't try to pull or direct the dog; all you want to do now is to acquaint him with this limited check on his freedom. The secret here, as in all training, is to remember to talk to him. At first he may be confused about his role. If he strains at the lead or chews on it, correct him by saying No. If he persists, accompany No with a quick jerk on the lead. As soon as he understands what you expect, he'll try to comply, because dogs, like children, basically want to please you. When he is good, let him know by scratching his ears and praising him.

Training to the lead should begin early. The new pup first learns to wear a leather collar, then to walk on a loose lead.

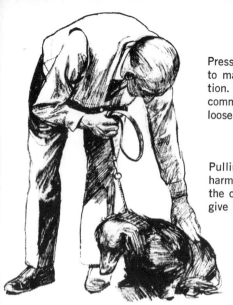

Press down on the dog's hindquarters to make him sit from a standing position. Accompany the action with the command Sit. The pup should be on a loose lead.

Pulling up by loose neck skin is a harmless way to raise a lazy puppy to the correct "sit" position. Remember to give the command, Sit, at same time.

Learning to Sit

Next, your dog must learn to sit at your command. Again, this is a puppy exercise, so have patience with him. Stand stationary, holding the lead in one hand. As you say *Sit*, press down on his hindquarters with the other hand. If the dog lies down instead, grasp the loose skin at his neck as shown in the illustration above and pull up until he is sitting (this won't hurt him). Repeat the command *Sit*. Since you have now added another word to his vocabulary, don't confuse the puppy by varying the command—and don't weaken it by also using his name. Praise him as soon as he sits. By the time your pup is three months old, he should have mastered this exercise. Now he will be ready to learn the more advanced lessons that follow.

16

FIRST FORMAL TRAINING

Sit–Stay Command

PRELIMINARY. The most important exercise you can teach your dog is to sit and stay on command. Once he learns this, you can leave him anywhere and know he will be there when you return. Wait until he is at least three months old before beginning the sit–stay. Your puppy should now recognize his name, be familiar with the lead and respond to the simple command *Sit*.

Use a longer lead (6 to 8 feet) than normal so that you and the dog can move freely. Holding the slack loosely in the right hand, walk the dog briefly, then bring him in as close to your left foot as possible. Give the command *Sit*. As soon as he sits, reward him by stroking his head (don't pat—few dogs appreciate being thumped on the head).

Now shift the lead to the other hand and swing forward in a half-circle so that you are facing the dog. Give the command *Stay*. At the same time bring your right hand—fingers together, palm forward—to the dog's nose to block his moving ahead. Keep all motions smooth. If your pup drops his head, repeat *Stay* and tap him lightly under his chin. Follow by again bringing your hand to his nose.

Avoid excessive correction by anticipating your dog's errors and rewarding him *before* he has time to commit them. In this way he will associate pleasure with doing what you want. Repeat several times, then let the pup romp briefly before undertaking the remainder of the exercise.

INTERMEDIATE. Once your dog has mastered the preliminaries, he must learn to remain in the stay position even when you are not present. Repeat the initial exercise. Then, with the lead in your left hand, straighten to a standing position and walk slowly around the dog. If he stands too, start again. Help him by repeating the command *Stay*, being careful not to confuse him by jerking or pulling on the lead.

Preliminary sit–stay begins with the dog in the sit position. Face the dog, holding the lead in your left hand. On the command Stay, bring your palm to his nose, preventing any break from the sit position.

The intermediate stage begins with the dog in the initial sit–stay position. Holding the lead loosely above his head for minimum control, walk slowly in a circle, repeating the command Stay whenever necessary.

The final stage introduces the dog to working off lead. On Stay, walk away, reinforcing the command by moving your arm toward the dog to stop him from breaking or following.

FINAL. Now drop the lead and go through the exercise exactly as before. As you move around the dog, increase each circle until you are about 10 feet away from him. After a rest, again run through the initial sit-stay, only this time, instead of walking around the dog, turn away from him and walk about 5 feet. Watch him over your shoulder, saying *Stay* when necessary. With each successive run-through, increase the distance between you and the dog until you can actually leave the room without his moving. It will take at least four training sessions and a maximum of patience to teach your dog this exercise. But once he has learned it, you will be able to leave him alone, in a parked car, in somebody else's home—or anywhere—with the confidence that he will stay on your command.

Walking at Heel

Taking your dog for a walk should be fun for you and for him. If certainly won't be if he pulls and fights on the lead or—if he is a big dog—literally drags you behind him. Nor does he have to be a show dog to learn to walk at heel obediently in about three lessons.

Walking briskly to sustain the dog's interest, hold the lead loosely in your right hand. Keep your left hand on the lead near the collar to help guide the dog as you vocally encourage him to heel.

Begin with the dog in a sit position on your left. With the end of the lead in your right hand, put your left hand close to his collar to direct him. On the command *Heel*, walk forward. A fast pace will keep the dog alert and his attention from wandering. When you stop, say *Sit* immediately and follow with praise.

Once your dog learns this much, he will no longer need the guidance of your hand near his collar. If you have a large breed, such as the Rhodesian ridgeback being trained in the illustration above, use a chain choke-collar during training to prevent his breaking away from you.

Keep the dog close to your left side as you walk. Always maintain a firm grip with both hands on the lead, but do not hold it taut. Should the dog lunge forward, one short jerk on the lead is much more effective than a long, weak pull. If he continues to pull, stop, bring the lead up short, and say *No*. Enforce this correction when necessary by slapping across the forequarters with the end of the lead.

Never let any dog, especially a big dog, intimidate or take advantage of you. And always remember that tone of voice in correction is more important than volume. Your dog will be happier, and so will you, when he learns to obey your commands.

Jerking sharply on the lead when the dog breaks, the trainer in this drawing shows the best hand position for maximum control during advanced stage of exercise, and relaxed lead on choke-collar.

Reward the dog at the end of the heel exercise by bringing him to the sit position close to your left leg. Stroke his head to show approval.

In persuading the dog to stay when down, you combine hand movement with the command Stay, keeping all movements slow and your voice gentle to avoid exciting or confusing the dog.

To help the dog to stay when standing, hold your hand against the inside leg joint and, when necessary, pull the dog up by the lead.

Down and Stand–Stay

Your dog now knows how to sit and stay on command. Teaching him to stay when lying down or standing follows naturally. To make him lie down, begin in the sit position. On the command *Down*, press on his shoulders with one hand as you motion him down with the other. Face him when you do this, so he knows you are not going to hurt him. If he remains sitting, repeat the command *Down* as you pull his forelegs toward you. This will make him lie down. As soon as he does, give the command *Stay*. Praise him immediately. To teach your dog to stay when standing, walk him on a loose lead, then stop and give the command *Stand*, followed by *Stay*. Prevent him from sitting by putting your hand against the joint of his hind leg as shown above. You may have to help him by looping the lead under his hindquarters and pulling upward as you give the commands.

24

Come Command

The most neglected training exercise is teaching your dog to come when you call him. The frustration of trying to get your dog's attention by shouting, whistling or rapping a spoon on his bowl can be avoided if you teach him the command *Come* as soon as he completes his basic training. Put your dog in the sit–stay position. With a long lead held loosely in one hand, walk a few feet away and face him, bending slightly forward. If your dog is small, instead of bending forward, squat down so that you are closer to his level. Any variation on a training method that helps your dog to understand better what you expect of him makes the exercise more enjoyable. On the command *Come*, jerk sharply on the lead. When he comes to you, stroke his

A leather collar is adequate for a thoroughly obedient dog at this stage of training.

Beginning the exercise, put your dog in a basic sit–stay position. Holding lead loosely, walk away, then face him and bend slightly toward him.

Following through, jerk the lead on the command Come. As soon as the dog obeys the command and comes to you, he should be rewarded with praise.

head and praise him. Each time you run through the exercise, increase the distance you walk from the dog. Then drop the lead and repeat. If he tries to follow you or starts to break before your command, instead of reprimanding him, say *Come* immediately. With a minimum of correction, he will learn faster and associate fun with the exercise.

PRACTICAL DISCIPLINE

Car Chasing

Young puppies are inclined to chase anything that moves. As they grow older this tendency often turns to chasing cars. Your dog won't understand that a car means danger unless you teach him. If he has never chased a car, the best way to ensure that he never will is to make him afraid of all cars. Fear, like praise, has a specific role in training. For this lesson you need a piece of split bamboo, which combines a loud, cracking noise with a harmless but stinging blow when you strike the dog.

Holding the lead firmly in one hand, walk your dog up to a car. When he is close to it, strike first the fender of the car and then the dog's chest with the bamboo. Make

A training aid of split bamboo is useful in all discipline, since it combines a loud noise with a stinging but harmless blow. The basis of corrective training is developing in your dog an association between unpleasant experience and forbidden object.

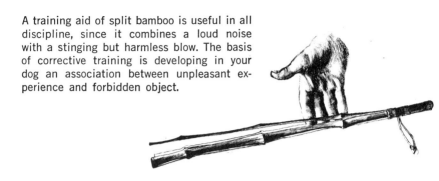

this a single motion from car to dog. At the same time say *No* and jerk sharply on the lead.

If your dog is a confirmed car chaser, you can try the above method, but you will probably find that more severe measures are necessary. The recommended method here can be dangerous, so put two collars and two leads on your dog to prevent his breaking free. You will also need two assistants—one to drive a car and the other to sit in the back seat armed with several tin cans filled with pebbles. Take

To prevent car chasing, deliberately instill a fear of autos in your dog. Walk him on a lead close to a car, strike a fender, then the dog with a piece of bamboo on the command *No.*

a firm grip on both leads close to the collars as shown on the opposite page. When the car drives by, let your dog begin to chase it. Then, on the command *No*, jerk sharply on the leads. At the same time have your assistant throw one or more of the tin cans at the dog. You may have to repeat this lesson several times, but it is one that your dog must learn. Until he does, no training measure is too severe when weighed against the injuries that sooner or later befall car chasers.

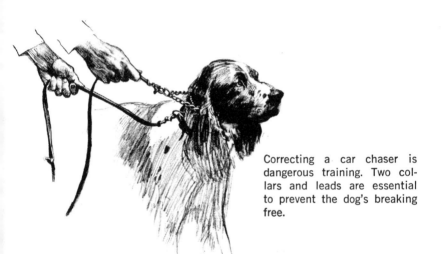

Correcting a car chaser is dangerous training. Two collars and leads are essential to prevent the dog's breaking free.

Manners

The easiest way to ensure good manners in your dog is to prevent his developing bad ones. Few dogs disobey deliberately, but unless you show them differently, they are apt to follow their wild ancestors' habits, which do not fit in with the jet age. While the following exercises are geared to grown dogs, it is not too soon to start an eight-week-old puppy on a modified form of the same routines. Make the exercise training periods short, not more than 2 or 3

28

minutes at a time. Do them often—eight to ten times a day is not too much, since the pup will learn by repetition—and do them in the house, since this is where you want him to behave.

Also, there is less distraction indoors for the learning puppy, and you do not have to stop, put on your hat and coat and go outside to train the dog. Use a very light plastic or leather collar and a very light cloth lead (a piece of seam binding or bias tape would be adequate). The pup should not feel weighted down or restrained.

Take your dog out of his playpen on the leash and walk him around the kitchen. Make him sit and stay in front of every door in the room. While he is sitting, open and shut the doors. He is off to a good start by not jumping on visitors and not running out each time a door is opened. Include kitchen cabinet doors if they are at his level, the icebox door, the closet door and any other inside door. Save doors that open to the outside until last, since they present the greatest temptation. Do not try them until the second or third practice session.

Using the heeling exercise, walk him around on the leash through all the rooms on the first floor. Make him heel as he goes; then praise him and put him back in his playpen. He is learning not to run and race in the house and to stay off the furniture, since you are showing him, through the heeling exercise, how you want him to act inside. You have never given him an opportunity to find out he can run and jump in these rooms.

If you have a grown dog who already does these things, go back to puppy training with him. Keep him out of the rooms unless you are there with him on lead. Do your obedience exercises with him just as if he were a puppy. Make him sit in front of the doors, make him heel around the rooms, and you will soon replace the bad habits with the good ones. Insist that the puppy or grown dog sit every time he comes to you. This will prevent his jumping on you and it's wonderful exercise (like push-ups for people).

29

The more he does it, the firmer his abdominal muscles and his rear legs become. This is particularly helpful in the puppy. The rapid development of these muscles will give him better control and his housebreaking will progress more rapidly.

All puppies like to chew things, and some have expensive tastes. Give your pup something of his own to chew on. When he chooses something of yours instead, reprimand him. If he still refuses to give up the object, put your hand, as shown in the drawing below, over his muzzle with your forefinger and thumb just above his lip so they exert pressure on his canine teeth. This way he will not be able to bite you and will be forced to let you take the object from his mouth. Say *Give* in a stern tone. It's not necessary to break a dog's spirit to make him behave. If you show him what you want of him, correct him as soon as he does wrong and reward him when he obeys you, all of his habits can be good ones.

Chewing things is common in young pups. If your dog refuses to drop an object on command No, put your hand over his muzzle so that your forefinger and thumb exert pressure on his canine teeth, enabling you to remove the object from his mouth.

Stage 1 in teaching your dog to heel off lead begins with passing the lead behind you and holding it loosely in your right hand. The left hand is used for initial guidance.

ADVANCED FORMAL TRAINING

Heel Off Lead

The most challenging test of your dog's obedience to your commands comes when you introduce him to walking without a lead. Work alone with him in an enclosed area so that he won't be distracted or run away. Romp with him briefly; then, using the lead, review his past lessons to make sure he knows them perfectly. With your dog in sit position, take the lead around your back and hold it in your right hand as shown above. Give the command *Heel*. Remember to walk briskly to keep his attention. Until now your dog has been used to being controlled by the lead, so if he doesn't follow you the first few times, guide him by holding his collar. Next, hang the lead loosely over your left arm and repeat the exercise. At first your dog may not walk as close to you as you want, but right now obedience is more important than precision. The object is to make him

Stage 2 further reduces control of the lead over the dog. Loop the lead over your arm and direct the dog by vocal command only.

Stage 3 simulates off-lead work as you drape the lead over your shoulder for minimum control. Obedience is more important here than precision.

heel with minimum guidance from the lead. When he does, praise him. Then reduce the lead control even more by draping it over your right shoulder. Repeat the exercise. Your dog should now be ready to walk off lead. Keep the detached lead in your hand. If he breaks, correct him immediately by slapping him on the rump. Always begin in the sit position, and make the command *Heel* forceful. This new freedom may confuse your dog at first, so be patient and praise him liberally when he obeys. Once he learns this lesson, you will be proud to take him anywhere.

SIMPLE TRICKS

Beg

All dogs enjoy showing off. You can enjoy it, too, by teaching yours a few tricks. To make him beg, begin in a sit position. On the command *Beg*, raise him by the front legs with one hand so that he sits up. With the other hand, lift his chin as shown below and repeat command *Beg*. If your dog has trouble keeping his balance at first, support his back against a wall. Once he is sitting up, praise him liberally. This is a good time to introduce a small tidbit as reward.

Teaching to beg begins in the sit position. On the command Beg, lift your dog's front leg and chin, then steady him until he regains his balance.

Roll Over

To make him roll over, put him in a down position. Pull his far foreleg toward you with one hand as you push his shoulder away from you with the other. At the same time, command *Roll over*.

Teaching your dog to roll over begins with the down position. On command Roll over, pull the dog's far foreleg toward you, at same time push his shoulder away.

Pray

You can teach him to pray by having him sit in front of a chair. On the command *Pray*, lift his forefeet up so that they rest on the edge of the chair, and press his head down gently on his paws. Here, as in all training, you must associate one clear concise command with the lesson you want your dog to learn. And he will enjoy learning new lessons if his reward is immediate and enthusiastic praise.

Fetch

Teaching to fetch is useful exercise, which can be combined with breaking your dog of chewing things. Open his mouth as shown on page 30. On command *Fetch*, put a rolled piece of paper between his teeth (below, left). Remove your hand and reward him with praise. Then cup your hand and hold it in front of him as you command *Give*. If he refuses, open his mouth until the paper drops into your hand, then reward. As soon as he understands what you want, hold the paper in front of him and command *Fetch*. Repeat, moving the paper farther away. Now you are ready to teach him to retrieve.

Intermediate stage in retrieving is taught on lead. First, guide your dog over a bench.

RETRIEVING ON COMMAND

Once your dog becomes used to fetching a rolled paper, he can learn to retrieve any object. You will appreciate this lesson when you drop something or want him to fetch your evening paper or slippers. Begin with the dog on lead for maximum control. At this stage you can substitute a glove or slipper for the rolled paper. With the dog in sit position, drop the object on the ground a few feet from him. Command *Fetch*. Reinforce the command by pointing at the object if your dog seems confused. As soon as he picks it up, say *Come*. When he returns to you, command *Give*, then praise him so that he knows you are pleased. Throw the object farther away from him each time. When he knows this stage thoroughly, turn a bench on its side as shown above and put the object on one side. Holding the lead loosely in your left hand, make the dog sit next to you on the near side of the bench. On the command *Fetch*, walk briskly forward and over the bench. If the dog hesitates, direct him by pulling slightly on the lead. When he picks up the object, lead him back over the bench, command *Sit*, then *Give*. Next, send him over the bench alone.

On the command Fetch, send the dog over the bench alone.

From here, it is just a matter of practice to teach him to jump higher barriers. And you needn't worry about his jumping the fence when you're away if he has learned to act on your command. In fact, if you train your dog to obey and respect you at all times, you will never have to worry about him at all.

Final stage finds the dog willing to jump high fences to retrieve any object on command. If your dog has learned obedience, he will only jump when ordered.

2
Field Dogs

MOST hunters who have ever owned gun dogs agree that with few exceptions these dogs also make fine house pets. More surprising, perhaps, is the fact that many house pets make excellent gun dogs without losing any of the qualities which endear them to the family at home. In the next four chapters, experts offer instructions in the training of field dogs. Photographs of the seventeen most popular sporting breeds appear in Chapter 7.

Before receiving field training, each dog should, of course, learn the simple rules of living with people. When he has mastered the commands to sit, to stay, to come when called, he is ready to take to the field.

THE FLUSHING SPANIELS

Springer spaniels are especially adaptable to the dual role of hunting and home companions. American and English cocker spaniels and English springer spaniels, in particular, are easy to teach, eager to learn and generally enthusiastic by nature. Given proper training, almost any spaniel can fulfill both roles and add immeasurably to his master's enjoyment. For most spaniels, the right age will be between six and nine months. Up to a year and a half, the average dog can still be taught to hunt, but much beyond this age training may be more difficult.

The flushing spaniel is perhaps the most versatile of all the sporting breeds, performing a triple job in the field. Not only will he find game; he will also flush it to the gun and retrieve it. The flushing spaniel seeks his game close to the hunter and within shotgun range. This characteristic, combined with a natural retrieving instinct, makes him a special favorite of the pheasant and grouse shooter who likes to hunt his birds on foot and at a reasonable pace.

THE TRAILING HOUNDS

The basset hound, black and tan coonhound and beagle are the most popular trailing hounds in America today; but in addition to these dogs, countless mixed strains are used for tracking. Most often, they follow rabbits, but these plodding and determined trackers also trail raccoons, foxes, deer and sometimes even people. Regardless of quarry, all of the trailing hounds share one trait—an extraordinary ability to follow a ground trail by scent. They must be taught, nonetheless, to concentrate their superior ability on a single scent and to follow it without interruption, no matter what other scents may cross the trail. This is the basis of all hound training, whether the dog be a basset after a rabbit or a bloodhound helping to rescue a lost child.

The amenable, relaxed, almost lazy disposition of the hound has made him so adaptable as a family pet that in recent years he has spent more time indoors and less in the field. Yet the qualities that made him such a good pet are combined with a superior nose and surprising physical endurance, qualifying the hound as a steadfast hunting expert. The desire to hunt is a powerful instinct in all hounds, and even the most sluggish family dog can become a good trailer.

THE RUGGED RETRIEVERS

The most rugged of all the sporting dogs, retrievers are specially equipped, both physically and temperamentally, for their strenuous job. In this country, the most popular are Chesapeake Bay, curly-coated, golden and Labrador retrievers, Irish water spaniel and poodle. All of these breeds are built for rough work in the outdoors, and specifically for use in duck and goose shooting.

Once a bird has been downed, the retriever is expected to locate it, regardless of where it has fallen, and deliver it to the hunter. Fine eyesight and a steady, determined disposition help the retriever do his job; but his most important features are his dense waterproof coat, heavy muscular structure and superb swimming ability, which enable him to work under the most adverse outdoor conditions. In fact, many retrievers actually seem to be at their best in freezing temperatures, icy winds and storm-tossed seas. For duck and goose hunters—especially northern hunters who shoot over water—retrievers can be excellent hunting companions, and, equally important, they can contribute a great deal to conservation by preventing the waste of crippled and lost birds.

THE POINTING DOGS

The desire to point is instinctive and exists to a limited degree in all dogs. In the pointing breeds, however, it has been specifically developed and intensified over the years.

These dogs have further been bred for speed and physical stamina to enable them to hunt quickly and skillfully over vast areas of game cover. The Brittany spaniel, Weimaraner, Vizsla and German shorthair are relative newcomers to the American hunting scene; the Irish, Gordon and English setters are oldtime favorites now making a comeback in the field after years of overbreeding for show. They have the same natural instinct for finding birds as the pointer, who has dominated quail shooting for decades.

The pointing dog's job is to work out ahead of the hunter and when he smells game literally to point it out to the man who follows him. One of the most dramatic experiences for a hunter in the field is the sight of a dog on point, his body tense and rigid, his nose extended in the direction of game. Once the pointing dog is frozen in this attitude, he will remain for a minute or an hour, if need be, while the hunter moves up to flush the bird. For the upland bird shooter, particularly the quail hunter, whether he seeks his game on horseback or on foot, a pointing dog is certainly his most valuable companion.

In training any breed of field dog, the bywords for the trainer are *practice* and *patience*. Flushing spaniels, trailing hounds, rugged retrievers and pointing dogs must be carefully trained before they can be expected to do a good job in the field. It is important to remember that dogs, like people, are individuals; some learn more quickly than others.

With practice and patience, training can be for the hunter, as well as the dog, a rewarding and exciting experience. Moreover, trainers frequently find that a dog becomes a better companion at home when he has learned to be a companion afield.

3
The
Flushing Spaniels
By Stanley MacQueen

FIRST TIME IN THE FIELD

THE OPENING PHASE of field training is easy and very informal. It involves no more than taking the young dog out in the field as often as possible to acquaint him with all types of terrain and game cover. A spaniel is born with a natural desire to hunt. Your job is to encourage this "birdiness," as it is called, by making his outdoor sessions fun. Keep them short—a half-hour every day rather than several consecutive hours once a week—and stop them, for a few days if necessary, when the dog seems to be tired or losing interest. The basic equipment you will need is a collar and lead, a whistle (police variety) and a .22-caliber blank training pistol.

Always take the dog afield on the lead, and before releasing him make him sit so that he understands you are the boss.

A training pistol accustoms the pup to gunfire in the field.

Short runs acquaint the puppy with thickets and brush.

A shallow pond for splashing introduces him to water.

Let him run free for a few minutes while he works off excess energy; then walk along in the direction he takes. When he gets too far ahead of you, call him back. Each time you call him, follow the command with several short whistle blasts. Eventually he will learn to associate this whistle signal with the voice command *Come*. If he is slow at first, be patient and avoid excessive correction. It is more important now for him to develop interest in a variety of cover than to obey every command. If he is reluctant to enter heavy brush or briers, encourage him by going in first. When you come to water, let him splash and play in it.

After the dog has been afield several times, accustom him to the sound of gunfire by shooting the training pistol in the air. Make sure he is at least 100 yards away from you the first few times you fire so that you don't startle him. Gradually decrease the distance as he becomes used to the noise.

When you are ready to leave the field for home, reward the pup with stroking and praise as you put him back on the lead. Remember that the most important part of this early training is to make it fun for the dog. It will be if every session afield is relaxed and short.

Praise is the best reward at the end of a session afield.

FIRST ENCOUNTER WITH BIRDS

As soon as the pup is ranging freely, sniffing eagerly for signs of game and entering all kinds of cover with boldness, he is ready for his first encounter with birds. At this stage it is not important that they be pheasants or grouse; pigeons are cheaper and easier to handle. Clip the flight feathers from one wing of a pigeon to prevent it from flying. Hold

Let the puppy sniff the bird to acquaint him with the game scent.

Encourage the dog to find the bird and bring it back to you.

the bird in your hand and let the dog sniff and nuzzle it. Then shake it slightly—this won't hurt the bird but will dizzy it so that it stays in one spot—and throw it a few feet away from you. Encourage the dog to go after the pigeon by moving your arm toward it and saying *Fetch*. He will probably pick it up right away, but he may decide to play with it. It is better to let him do so briefly the first few times rather than risk souring him on birds by correcting him. As soon as he takes the bird in his mouth, whistle him to you. If he returns without the bird, repeat *Fetch* and encourage him by whistle and voice to bring it. When he does, reward him. Repeat this exercise daily, planting the bird farther away each time. And remember, be patient with his mistakes and generous with praise.

Control begins with a single whistle blast meaning Sit.

BEGINNING CONTROLS

After the dog has some field experience behind him and is used to retrieving live birds, he is ready for the basic exercises that will control him when hunting. Hand and whistle

Command is reinforced by hand and voice signals.

commands are the tools with which you exercise control. The whistle is actually a substitute for the voice commands he has learned at home; in the field it is more valuable than the voice because it carries farther and with more authority. The dog already knows that a series of short blasts means *Come*. The next and more formal whistle command is the sit–stay. Begin with the voice command *Sit–stay*. Follow it immediately with a single, sharp whistle blast and reinforce it by holding your hand, palm toward the dog, as shown on page 47. Move slowly away, steadying him with your hand and repeating the single whistle blast if he tries to follow you. Once he masters this command—and it may require weeks of training—he will stop and sit to the whistle whenever he hears it.

FIELD DIRECTIONS

A flushing dog must stay within range of the gun (not more than 40 to 50 yards from you) and hunt all cover around you. On the previous page you learned how to stop him by whistle anywhere in the field. The next step is to send, or cast, him off to hunt in another direction. Begin with the dog in the sit position. Send him to the left or the right by moving your arm and body in that direction. Accompany the arm signal with *two* short whistle blasts. The double whistle blast is used to send the dog in any direction; the arm signal indicates the direction he is to go. As the dog ranges ahead of you, whistle him to stop. Then, with your arm and whistle, cast him in a new direction. Repeat the signals daily until he understands them. When he does, you will be able to control the distance he ranges and the area he hunts.

Arm signals direct the puppy; the whistle sends him to hunt.

Cast the dog to the right with your arm motion.

Outward movement of your hand sends the dog ahead.

FLUSHED BIRDS

When you have acquired control of the way your dog ranges in the field—this takes two to three months of daily training—he is ready for the final exercise before an actual hunt: response to a flushed bird. This is called steadying the dog to wing and shot. Use a scented dummy instead of a bird for this training. At first the dog will be easier to handle on a check rope. Holding the rope loosely, whistle the dog to sit. Throw the dummy in front of him and fire the training pistol. If he starts after the dummy, repeat the single whistle blast and pull sharply on the rope. The

The check rope, looped loosely at the dog's neck, prevents him from breaking.

dog should remain steady until you give the signal to retrieve. Repeat the exercise, gradually moving farther away from the dog. Each time, throw the dummy closer to him. This will tempt the spaniel to break. If he does, correct him immediately. Remove the rope only when he is steady. This is one of the difficult exercises to teach, but when the dog learns it, he is ready to go hunting.

Throw the dummy close to the dog to simulate a flushed bird.

The dog must retrieve only upon command.

Teaching control is easier if a
friend does the shooting.

THE HUNT

The most fun and the most interesting part of training a
spaniel for the field begins when you take him out after
live game. It can also be a trying time for the novice trainer
because his dog must face a number of new experiences.
This will be the young spaniel's first encounter with birds
that fly, with a shotgun, which makes a louder noise than
a training pistol, and with having birds shot over him. You
can make it easier for the dog, and give yourself more
freedom to control him, if you take along a friend to do the
shooting. A .410 shotgun on the first few hunts will also
be less startling than a bigger, noisier gun like a 12-gauge.
Pigeons are still the least expensive birds to use during these
first shooting sessions. Before taking the dog into the field,
dizzy several pigeons and plant them at intervals in the
cover. Then with your friend walking slightly apart from,
but abreast of you, start the dog hunting. You will have
greater control over him if you limit his range to a maximum
of 30 yards at first. Be on the alert at all times for signs of

The dog should sit or "hup" as soon as a bird flushes.

game. As soon as the dog flushes a bird, whistle him to sit. This is called hupping to the game. Although he should automatically do this now, he may forget at the sight of a flushed bird. Anticipate such a mistake by using the whistle command as often as necessary. The dog should remain steady in the hup position while your friend shoots the bird. Then send the dog after it. When he has had some experience on pigeons, take him to a natural game area or shooting preserve to acquaint him with pheasants. And don't expect even the brightest dog to be an expert right away. He will become one only with practice.

The spaniel must remain steady while the hunter shoots the bird.

HIGH POINT

The reward of these training sessions afield and the high point of the hunt will come when your spaniel retrieves his first wild bird and brings it triumphantly to you. This is the climax of the months you have worked with him in the field, and it is also the moment when a sportsman realizes that, besides a pet, he owns a useful and intelligent gun dog. When you whistle him back after the bird has been downed, remember that the dog will expect and deserve some praise from you. Give it to him enthusiastically, because now he is a hunter and has earned it.

4
The
Trailing Hounds
By Fred Huyler

GAME HOUNDS

TRAILING hounds—beagles, bassets and coonhounds—must learn to concentrate on a single track before they are ready to go on a real hunt. And since these breeds are small-game hunters, a game trail instead of a human trail is used in training them. For this early training, it will be much easier for both you and the dog if you make an artificial trail, which you do by saturating a bag of sawdust with commercial game scent and dragging it about 100 yards. Then, with the dog on lead, take him to the place where the trail starts. When he locates the scent, encourage him to follow it and correct him if he wanders. At the end of the trail, reward him with praise and a tidbit. When he has learned to follow an easy trail, remove the lead and drag the scent through brush and briers so that he gets used to more difficult routes. Spend at least two months on this stage of training.

55

Take the dog on lead to the place where the artificial trail begins.

FIRST ENCOUNTER WITH GAME

As soon as the dog can follow an artificial trail, he is ready for live game. At this stage the type of game—regardless of what the dog will eventually hunt—is not important as long as it leaves a simple, obvious trail. A rabbit from a pet shop is easy to care for and slow enough for a young dog to keep up with. This training should take place in an enclosed area so both the game and the dog are under control. Let the dog sniff the rabbit while a friend holds it. Then take the dog out of sight and release the rabbit. Unleash the dog and encourage him to find and follow the rabbit's trail. An older dog can help in this training by leading the way. In any case, stay close behind so you can separate the dogs and the rabbit if necessary. Take the dog out with the rabbit for about a week and keep the sessions short so that the dog will not lose his enthusiasm.

56

Let the dog set the pace as he follows the scent along the trail.

The dog sniffs the rabbit to become acquainted with the scent.

The rabbit is released and the dog sets out on chase.

FIRST TIME IN THE FIELD

The most challenging phase of hound training occurs when you go afield after wild game. Now the trail may lead anywhere; it may be old or it may not exist at all. But the measure of a good trailing hound is experience, and the only way he will gain it is by hunting as often as possible. Again, an older dog can be of help during these sessions because the young dog will follow him and learn by imitation. Whether you take the dog afield alone or with another dog, however, always take him on lead so that he knows you are the boss. When you reach the hunting area, release the dog and encourage him to start hunting by talking to him as

On the first hunt, bring an older dog along as a guide for your pup.

Try to keep close to the dog and use a light-gauge gun.

you walk through the woods. Many people find the chase itself so enjoyable that they never shoot over their trailing hounds. Nevertheless, it is a good idea to acquaint your dog with gunfire so that he will not be frightened by it. You can do this by carrying along a shotgun (a .410 is better than a larger gauge at first because it makes less noise) and firing it from time to time when the dog is actually on a trail and at least 50 yards from you. In areas where game is scarce or cover is dense, beat the bushes with a stick as you walk along. Rabbits and other small game often sit tight at the approach of danger and can sometimes be routed out of hiding by such action. And always be on the alert for signs of game. You may see an animal take off before the dog is able to scent it. If you do, call him back to you and help him locate the trail.

Beat the bushes with a stick to drive out hidden game.

Show the dog the place where a game trail begins.

RUNNING A FRESH TRAIL

When you locate a fresh game trail, the pup will probably bound off on the scent, particularly if there is an older dog along. If he does not, start him on the trail by pointing out the way. You will know he is on scent when you hear the deep-throated baying that all game hounds instinctively sound when they hit a fresh track. This is the climax of the chase and the reward for the many hours of training. For whether you hunt with a gun or for the chase alone, the musical cry of a tracker closing in on his quarry is one of the most exciting sounds in the field.

The young dog takes lead from the older dog in following the trail.

5

The

Rugged Retrievers

By James A. Cowie

EARLY FIELD TRAINING

A RETRIEVER is born with an instinct to fetch, and he usually shows signs of it by playfully picking up any object thrown to him. This does not mean that he is ready to start his formal field training. You may actually discourage his natural instincts if you try to train him too early. Most dogs are not ready until they are about nine months old. Some Labradors can be started sooner, but Chesapeakes and goldens often do better when training begins at eleven or twelve months. Until this time, take the pup out every day (or as often as possible) for runs of no more than fifteen minutes and just introduce him to the outdoors. Walk with him through fields and brush so that he gets used to varied terrain. Let him play with a glove by throwing it to him. When he picks it up, call him back to you by blowing several short, soft blasts on a training whistle.

Blow the whistle to call the pup to you as he retrieves the glove.

Praise him if he fetches it to you, but don't correct him if he does not. Your goal now is simply to acquaint him with the outdoors and with one simple whistle command.

FORMAL EXERCISES

When the pup is used to the outdoors and has learned the basic *sit*, *stay*, and *come* commands from his home training, he is ready to start formal work in the field. Begin by making him sit. Take hold of his collar and throw a training dummy about 10 yards. Release him on the command *Fetch*, and direct him toward the dummy with a sweeping movement of your arm. As soon as he picks up the dummy, whistle him back to you. If he runs the other way, don't chase after him. Instead, step back and call him by name. When he finally comes to you, be ready to take the dummy from him before he drops it. Spend several weeks on this exercise and ignore his mistakes.

Hold the dog in the sit position, then throw the training dummy.

Step back and take the dummy from him before he drops it.

With the dog on lead, command Sit and then throw the dummy.

GUNFIRE

After the pup has learned to fetch the dummy and deliver it to your hand, he must become accustomed to gunfire. For exercise, put the dog on a long lead and make him sit. Holding the end of the lead, step away from him. Then throw the dummy as far as you can and, while it is still in the air, fire a training pistol. If the dog breaks, jerk sharply on the lead, repeating the command *Sit*. When he is finally steady, drop the lead and command *Fetch*. Practice this exercise daily, correcting him if necessary, so that he learns to remain motionless until you send him to retrieve.

If the dog breaks at the sound of the pistol, pull sharply on lead.

BLIND RETRIEVES

In hunting, particularly from a blind, game often falls out of the dog's line of sight. He must learn, therefore, to find birds he did not actually see. The dog already knows that a series of short whistle blasts means *Come*. Now teach him that a single, short blast means *Stop*. Once he has mastered this command, have a friend plant the dummy out of the dog's sight. Send the dog straight ahead, then stop him by whistle. His instinct will be to look at you. When he does, call out, *Fetch*, and move your arm in the direction of the dummy. If he gets off course, stop him again and repeat the arm signal.

As soon as the dog is following your directions, substitute a dead bird for the dummy so that he becomes used to feathers and game scent. At this same stage of training, ask a friend to fire a shotgun from about 30 yards away each time you send the dog to retrieve. Have the friend move closer as the dog becomes accustomed to the noise of the gun. Spend about two months on this training.

The dog starts a blind retrieve by moving out on word Fetch.

He stops at the whistle, looks back for your arm signal.

He sets out in a new direction as you move arm, body.

WATER PRACTICE

Most retrievers are ready to start working in the water after about three months of formal field training. If the weather is very cold, however, it is better to wait a few months longer. The dog will not mind freezing water once he is used to it, but you may frighten him if you start him off with an ice-cold plunge. The best place to begin this training is a shallow pond with a firm, sandy bottom. (Avoid salt water because the dog may try to drink it.) Take the dog to the edge of the pond and, with your hand on his collar, make him sit. Throw the dummy about 10 yards out. Wait until it hits the surface, then command, *Fetch*. Most likely the dog will leap instinctively into the water. If he just paddles in, don't be discouraged—he soon will learn to leap. Occasionally a dog refuses to go in at all. If this should happen, have a friend throw the dummy while you stand in the water holding the dog's lead. On the command *Fetch*, pull the dog in and encourage him to swim to you. Once the dog is retrieving the dummy without difficulty, get a live duck and shackle his wings and feet by slipping an old sock with the toe cut out over his body. Then set the duck out about 20 yards from shore (a shackled duck can float well even though it cannot fly) and send the dog to fetch it. When the dog has made a few successful retrieves, set out some decoys so that he gets used to swimming through them.

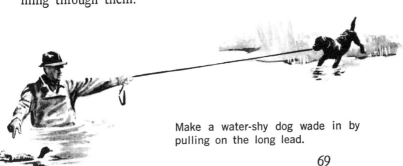

Make a water-shy dog wade in by pulling on the long lead.

Start the exercise by holding the dog in the sit position at the water's edge.

Next, send him into the water to retrieve a shackled duck.

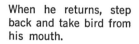

When he returns, step back and take bird from his mouth.

WORKING FROM A BLIND

Before the dog is ready to take hunting, he must become familiar with a shooting blind. It is not necessary to have an actual waterfowl blind or even water for this exercise. In fact, many people prefer the convenience of working their dogs in the back yard. Simulate a blind by setting up an enclosure of window screens or packing boxes. Leave an opening in the front or side big enough so that the dog can get in and out. Make him sit inside the blind. Throw the training dummy as far as you can and fire a shotgun in the air, then send the dog to fetch. If he hesitates about leaving the blind, repeat the command. Once he is out, direct him with hand and whistle signals. When he returns, encourage him to leap back into the blind, and correct him if he drops the dummy outside. This exercise, besides being vital training for a pup, is also excellent preseason preparation for an experienced dog.

Throw the training dummy from inside an artificial blind.

Fire the shotgun and send the dog through the opening to retrieve.

Make him return with the dummy through the opening in the blind.

Sit the dog behind logs to obstruct his view of the water.

WORKING BEHIND OBSTACLES

The next step is to test the dog under difficult conditions. Choose a pond or bay with an overgrown bank that obstructs the view of the water. Make the dog sit behind some logs or deadfalls and take hold of his collar so that you can control him. Have a friend fire a shotgun and then throw a shackled bird into the water where the dog cannot see it.

Send the dog over the logs and into the water to make the retrieve.

Send him to fetch it. If he tries to go around the logs rather than over them, pull him back by the collar and give the command again. Follow through with arm and whistle signals to direct him to the bird. He should return over the logs and deliver the bird to your hand. When he has mastered this obstacle training, he is ready to take out hunting.

RETRIEVING WILD BIRDS

The climax of your months of training comes when you take the dog hunting. This is a new and sometimes bewildering experience for him. It will be easier if you go out alone at first so that he is not distracted by other hunters and dogs. In the blind the dog should sit motionless beside you while you shoot. If he seems restless, stroke him occasionally to keep him quiet. When the first birds are down, your job is over and the dog's job really begins. It is

The dog must be steady in the blind while you fire at birds.

one he will enjoy, and if the dog is handled properly, the hunter, too, will derive deep satisfaction from watching a well-trained retriever return triumphantly with a bird that might otherwise have been lost.

The dog should grasp the bird firmly but gently as he makes the retrieve.

6

The Pointing Dogs

By Richard S. Johns

INTRODUCTION TO THE FIELD AND GUNFIRE

RECENT research into the canine mind has shown us that
a pup can absorb training at a much earlier age than we
once thought possible. Pups can and should be walked out
into the field starting at the age of three months or earlier
when possible. They should be encouraged to investigate all
strange sights, sounds and smells. At first a pup will do little
else but stay close to the person walking him, but in time a

Encourage your pup to explore
the outdoors.

Introduce your young dog to
gunfire.

good pup will get bolder and cast farther from his handler,
taking an active interest in small birds, butterflies or any
moving objects. Allow the pup to chase anything that will
help to build up his hunting desire and instill self-confidence.

When the puppy gets bolder, ventures farther from his
handler and is actively chasing small birds or game, the time
has come to introduce him to light gunfire. Carry a trainers
.22-caliber pistol, but use it cautiously. When the pup is out
about 40 yards, fire *one* time only. If he ignores the noise, fine.
If he returns to the handler, pay no attention, keep on walking. He should soon go on with his hunting. When another
far-off chase is under way, fire one time again. As time goes
on, more and more shots can be fired when the pup is pre-
occupied with his chases. A word of warning: There is a
common practice among the unknowing to take a small pup
to a trap shoot, skeet field or rifle range, thinking it a good
way to condition him to gunfire. *Don't!* There is nothing
worse to make a pup fearful of gunfire. He must be condi-
tioned to it by his associating it with the pleasure of chasing
game. If care and common sense are practiced, no pup
should ever be apprehensive of a gun's report.

76

During early field training, even a three-month-old pup can be taught to come in to a call or whistle, and to change direction by whistle and hand signal. A change of direction can be brought about by a sharp blast on the whistle to get the pup's attention, then wave your hand in the direction you wish the pup to go, and walk in that direction yourself. Later, change his course again in the same manner. In a short time the pup will respond quite well to this. A long, low blast can be used to bring him right in to the handler. This can be accomplished by such a whistle note accompanied by the voice. Care should be exercised not to overdo all this.

EARLY OBEDIENCE OR YARD TRAINING

Given a choice of but two commands for use in handling the pointing dog, most trainers would select *Come here* and *Whoa*. The reason for this will be clear in the following paragraphs on teaching a dog to *whoa* and to point.

The pup must have a thorough understanding of the *whoa* command, for the pointing dog must obey this command under all circumstances. Most of his advanced training will hinge on it.

To teach this the trainer needs a good, large-linked chain choke collar and a 6-foot leather or web leash. Take the pup to a quiet, level piece of ground. Have the pup in hand, walking to the side of the handler. In a clear voice, give the command of *Whoa*. With this the handler should stop, bringing the pup to a halt as he does. The pup must be kept standing as he stops. All efforts to move forward must be gently checked. The pup should be stroked upon his back and soothed with a low voice. At first do not keep the pup standing in this position more than 10 or 15 seconds. After that length of time the pup is given the order to move on, either by two short blasts on the whistle, or by the voice command, *Go on*. As the order to move on is given, the handler himself moves out. Walk the pup 10

To train your dog to whoa on command, use a large-linked chain choke collar and a long lead.

Stroke the pup gently on his back when he comes to a halt on command.

When you order him to Go on, move out with him.

Teach your pup to stand still when you move away from him.

or 15 feet, repeat the command Whoa and bring him to a stop. At first it is common for a pup to want to *sit* down. Never let him sit, under any circumstances, when under the order Whoa. In fact, *never* teach your young pointing dog to sit on command—this cannot be emphasized enough. Within a few days the pup will stop and stand quietly.

Now the handler stops the pup and makes his attempt to move about. He should step to the front of the pup, but with the hand quickly check any move on the pup's part to follow him. This procedure should be followed until such time as the handler can walk a complete circle around the standing pup without the pup's turning to follow or move in any way. As the pup progresses in this phase, he should be made to stand still for longer intervals and the handler should walk farther to the front of him. The handler should now tempt the pup to move by kicking at grass clumps, tossing a stone into the grass as if to flush game ahead of the dog. Each session the handler should walk more and more to the front and sides of the standing pup, in due time 100 feet or more, returning to the pup's side before sending him on. Soon the handler should be able to stop the pup on the Whoa command at any reasonable distance and expect him to remain stationary until sent on by command.

Tie a short cord to a leg of the chuckar partridge before placing it in nearby cover.

POINTING

In most of the pointing breeds, the instinct to point should come to the fore by the time the pup is from six to eight months of age. To some pups it comes earlier; to others, later. In all cases it is the handler's job to further develop the instinct that is there.

Use a chuckar partridge in the pointing sessions to follow. Quail can also be used, but the chuckar is a larger, tougher bird which can stand more handling and has a stronger flight. Secure a short, stout wrapping cord to its foot; fasten the other end to a 3-inch piece of wood. The handler will need a 30- to 50-foot check cord and a chain choke collar.

Have a helper take the bird to a large grass field that has sufficient cover to hide the bird. Let the chuckar beat its wings near the ground just before it is tucked into the grass so that scent is spread for the pup. The dog should not see the game put down. The handler attaches the long line to the dog and works him *upwind* in the direction of the planted bird. When the pup smells the bird he should stop and point. The handler restrains the pup and advances, soothing him, gently stroking his back and now and then nudging him forward. As slight pressure is put to the dog's quarters, the pup will hold, resist and become firmer on point. Dogs love to be handled like this when on point.

When the pup smells the bird,
he should stop and point.

Soothe and stroke your dog
and then nudge him forward.

When you apply this slight
pressure, he will become
firmer on point.

During the first few sessions don't keep the puppy pointing for more than 15 or 20 seconds. As the sessions continue, the puppy can be kept progressively longer on point. Now the helper can step ahead of the pup, pick the wood and string out of the grass and the bird will flush. As the bird flushes, the helper can fire the .22-caliber pistol. The handler commands his dog to *Whoa* and checks him up short if he attempts to give chase. Mark the chuckar's flight, noting the spot where it settled to the ground. Then swing the dog off the bird's line of flight and in a roundabout way, always with the wind in the pup's face, go for the chuckar again and repeat the same exercise. Three such performances per session are enough for the pup and the chuckar. Repeat this exercise often until the young dog is steady to point, wing and shot. Then it is time to work with wild game or released birds.

Flush the chuckar, fire your .22 and command your dog to whoa. Check him if he tries to break.

SHOOTING GAME OVER THE YOUNG DOG

Once the dog is made steady to wing and shot, he is ready for the game-shooting exercise. For this the handler needs a helper who is a good wing shot. A .410-gauge shotgun will serve the purpose well. The helper plants the chuckar (the string and stick are not used here) and the dog is brought upwind, as in previous sessions. But now the helper puts up the bird and fells it in view of the pointing dog. The handler gives the command to *Whoa* and holds the dog back with the rope if he attempts to break. The dog should be kept standing for a few seconds before being sent on to the bird.

When your helper shoots a bird, keep the dog standing for a few seconds before sending him to retrieve it.

Your pup should gently pick up the bird and return it to you.

Hopefully, he will pick it up and he should be encouraged to return it to the handler. If he refuses to do so, go out to the bird, toss it and coax the dog to pick it up. Use no force. If the dog eventually picks up the bird and gently returns it, you're in business. If the dog flatly refuses to pick up and carry game, he will have to be put through a course of retrieving.

HONORING OR BACKING A BRACEMATE'S POINT

After the dog has hunted birds for several months, he is ready to learn to "back," or honor, another dog's point. This is the finishing exercise in a bird dog's training. You will need the help of a friend and an experienced dog. Plant a bird and let the older dog point it. Then lead your dog on a rope up to within 5 feet of him. He may instinctively go on point when he sees the other dog. If he does not, stop him and help him into a point with your hands. When he is steady, have your friend flush and shoot the bird. Keep a grip on the dog's collar and talk to him so he doesn't break.

Repeat the exercise on lead until the dog knows what you expect of him; then practice off the lead, encouraging him to back at the sight of the other dog. Eventually he will honor a point from as far away as he can see it. For the bird shooter, there is probably no more thrilling sight in the field than that of one or more dogs frozen motionless as they back another.

Teach your dog to honor another dog's point.

7
A Gallery of Popular Field Dogs

THE FLUSHING SPANIELS

English Cocker Spaniel

English Springer Spaniel

Black and Tan Coonhound

THE TRAILING HOUNDS

Bloodhound

Basset Hound

Beagle

THE RUGGED RETRIEVERS

Irish Water Spaniel

Chesapeake Bay Retriever

Golden Retriever

Labrador Retriever

Pointer

THE POINTING DOGS

German Shorthair

Weimaraner

Vizsla

English Setter

THE POINTING DOGS

Irish Setter

Brittany Spaniel